THE VOCABULARY OF MIMI

AN ABRIDGED DICTIONARY
DEDICATED TO THE LYRICS OF
MARIAH CAREY

BYRON MCCRAY MILLER

Copyright © 2025 by Byron McCray Miller

All rights reserved. No part of this book may be reproduced in any form without permission from the author, except as permited by U.S. copyright law.

First paperback edition April 2025

ISBN (paperback): 978-1-7333488-1-2
ISBN (e-book): 978-1-7333488-2-9

Library of Congress Control Number: 2025905899

DEDICATION

This book is dedicated to my lambily
and to The Vocal Dictionary,
Mariah Carey.

— B.M.M.

> "CHALLENGE YOURSELF TO USE WORDS THAT PAINT A MORE VIVID PICTURE OF WHAT YOU'RE TRYING TO SAY.
>
> THESE NEW WORDS MIGHT EVEN INSPIRE NEW STORIES IN YOUR WRITING."
>
> — MARIAH CAREY

INTRODUCTION

This book is for the lambs, of which I am proud to be one.

From the first day that I heard "Vision of Love," I committed myself to a flock-like existence following the iconic journey of Mariah Carey. Since that day in May 1990, I knew that the soprano would be ever-present and intrinsic to my path. I became a *Mariahologist* — studying every performance, every cassette jacket or compact disc booklet (I'm aging myself), every mainstream song, every deep cut, and every note from the low F2 to the dolphin-pitched G7#. I've had the fortune of finding my fellow lambs throughout each era of my life, constantly reminded that Mariah's impact transcends race, age, gender identity and time.

Certainly the name "Mariah Carey" is synonymous with a celebrated career of achievement. Singer. Songwriter. Producer. Actress. Retailer. Philanthropist. Mother. More than 200 million albums sold. Nineteen *Billboard* Hot 100 chart number-one singles. Nineteen World Music Awards. Sixteen *Billboard* Music Awards. Five Grammy Awards. Ten American Music Awards. Three Guinness World Record titles. Oh, and a modern Christmas standard.

What has always positioned the record-breaking diva apart from her more traditional counterparts has been her insistence upon creative control over her narrative. Opting to be more than a vocal mouthpiece for songwriters to tell their stories, she ensures that she has a pen in the game as a co-writer and co-producer. She has not just survived but also thrived in the male-dominated music industry by curating collaborations on her own terms and in her own words.

Mariah's signature 8-octave vocal range, infectious melodies, glam squad, rainbows and butterflies often overshadow her possession of an equally distinguishable vocabulary. With writing credits on 18 of her 19 chart-toppers, the elusive chanteuse's penchant for storytelling has reigned since she penned her first number-one, "Vision of Love," at 17. Since that powerhouse debut, it has become a mark of the songbird to nestle an uncommon, ten-dollar word into each song. Whether coming back *incessantly* or being oh, so *acquiescent* — textured nouns, verbs, adjectives, and adverbs would become *vividly emblazoned* in our minds — adding layers to Carey's journaled migration across the genres of pop, R&B, hip-hop, dance and gospel.

If we were to acknowledge time (which Mariah does not), this abridged dictionary is more than 30 years in the making. Sharing this nostalgic collection of more than 250 decadent words that have been extracted from Carey's lyrics is my way of passing down all the unfamiliar words that a young, Black and gay lamb from Brooklyn, New York, scribbled on looseleaf sheets and in composition notebooks while patiently sitting beside his stereo – pressing the pause and play buttons alternately. I've learned volumes about the supreme songbird, but most importantly, I've learned volumes about my supreme self.

If you are intrigued by this book, it means that I am not alone. For decades, Mariah's polysyllabic treasures have elevated the writing, daily conversations and way of life of devoted lambs across the globe. Many have been on the joyride from the beginning, while younger generations have more recently discovered their safe space within the herd. No matter your entry point, you are "*lambily.*"

May you revel in *The Vocabulary of Mimi*. May this book serve as a literary companion to your discography. Above all, may you be uplifted by your expanded lexicon.

"*You'll finally see the truth — that a hero lies in you.*"

A NOTE TO THE LAMBS

You are invited to notate your newly discovered words from Mariah Carey's songbook on the lined pages in the back of this book.

A NOTE ON THE DEFINITIONS

Many of the words in this book have multiple meanings and pronunciations. Although it is recognized that they are by no means the only acceptable definitions and pronunciations, the meanings featured in this book are based on their context within Mariah Carey's lyrics.

A NOTE ON THE SOURCES

All definitions are sourced from dictionaries.
All words are extracted from the discography of Mariah Carey.

Mariah Carey, 1990
Emotions, 1991
MTV Unplugged, 1992
Music Box, 1993
Merry Christmas, 1994
Daydream, 1995
Butterfly, 1997
Number 1's, 1998
Rainbow, 1999
Glitter, 2001
Greatest Hits, 2001
Charmbracelet, 2002
The Remixes, 2003
The Emancipation of Mimi, 2005
E=MC², 2008
Memoirs of An Imperfect Angel, 2009
Merry Christmas II You, 2010
Me. I Am Mariah… The Elusive Chanteuse, 2014
Number 1 to Infinity, 2015
Caution, 2018
The Rarities, 2020

abandonment /əˈbandənmənt/ *noun*
an act or instance of leaving a person or thing permanently and completely
"Abandonment returns to taunt me again."
— "I Only Wanted", *Charmbracelet*

abundant /əˈbənd(ə)nt/ *adjective*
existing or available in large quantities; plentiful
"Everyday of my life's so abundant with joy."
— "Yours", *Charmbracelet*

abruptly /əˈbrəp(t)lē/ *adverb*
in a sudden or unexpected manner
"And it's too hard for me to leave abruptly / 'Cause you're the only thing I wanna do."
— "Honey", *Butterfly*

accentuate /akˈsen(t)SHəˌwāt/ *verb*
to make more noticeable or prominent
"It might benefit me to throw something on / To feature my hips, accentuate my ass, and steal the show."
– "Migrate", *E=MC2*

acquiescent /ˌakwēˈes(ə)nt/ *adjective*
willing to accept something without protest, or to do what someone else wants
"I was oh so acquiescent / But I learned my lesson."
— "It's A Wrap", *Memoirs of an Imperfect Angel*

affectionately /əˈfekSH(ə)nətlē/ *adverb*
in a way that displays or is characterized by fondness or tenderness
"But see it ain't just a physical thing / He's gotta treat me affectionately."
— "One and Only", *The Emancipation of Mimi*

alienation /ˌālēəˈnaSH(ə)n/ *noun*
the state or experience of being isolated from a group or an activity to which one should belong or in which one should be involved

> *"SUFFERED FROM **ALIENATION** / CARRIED THE WEIGHT ON MY OWN."*
> — "Vision of Love", *Mariah Carey*

alleviate /əˈlēvēˌāt/ *verb*
to make (something, such as pain or suffering) less severe
"It's just the feeling that comes over me / I cannot alleviate"
— "Want You", *Glitter*

aloof /əˈlo͞of/ *adjective*
removed or distant either physically or emotionally
"Time after time I reach for you / I try and I try, but you're so aloof."
— "Slipping Away", *Rarities*

ambiguous /amˈbigyəwəs/ *adjective*
open to or having several possible meanings or interpretations
"Ambiguous without a sense of belonging to touch / Somewhere halfway, feeling there's no one completely the same."
— "Outside", *Butterfly*

ambivalent /amˈbiv(ə)lənt/ *adjective*
having mixed feelings or contradictory ideas about something or someone
"I'll be that babygirl when you're immature / Don't be ambivalent towards me."
— "8th Grade", *Caution*

amid /əˈmid/ *preposition*
surrounded by; in the middle of
"We kissed under the sky, amid the city lights."
— "Lullaby", *Charmbracelet*

anguish /ˈaNGgwiSH/ *noun*
severe mental or physical pain or suffering
"Bitterness isn't worth clinging to after all the anguish we've all been through."
— "Sunflowers for Alfred Roy", *Charmbracelet*

apprehension /ˌaprəˈhen(t)SH(ə)n/ *noun*
anxiety or fear that something bad or unpleasant will happen
"My apprehension blew away, I only wanted you / to taste my sadness as you kissed me in the dark."
"The Roof", *Butterfly*

atrocities /əˈträsədēz/ *noun*
extremely wicked or cruel acts, typically involving physical violence or injuries
"There's a place up above / With no more hurt and struggling / Free of all atrocities and suffering."
"Fly Like a Bird", *The Emancipation of Mimi*

befriended /bəˈfrendəd/ *verb*
to form a bond with someone by offering help or support
"A boy and a girl befriended me / We're bonded through despondency."
— "Petals", *Rainbow*

bittersweet /ˈbidərˌswēt/ *adjective*
containing a mixture of sadness and happiness
"I'm suppressing the tears and it's bittersweet / 'Cause he's head over heels but it ain't that deep."
— "Crybaby", *Rainbow*

blatant /ˈblātnt/ *adjective*
completely lacking in subtlety; very obvious
"I can't be elusive with you, honey / 'Cause it's blatant that I'm feelin' you."
— "Honey", *Butterfly*

bountiful /ˈboun(t)əf(ə)l/ *adjective*
liberal or generous in bestowing gifts or favors
"I found my saving grace within you / And the bountiful things that you do."
— "My Saving Grace", *Charmbracelet*

camouflage /ˈkaməˌflä(d)ZH/ *verb*
to conceal the identity of something by modifying its appearance
"I camouflage my tears / And you wear your disguise."
— "Camouflage", *Me. I Am Mariah…The Elusive Chanteuse*

captivates /ˈkaptəˌvāts/ *verb*
to attract and hold the interest and attention of; charm
"It captivates my mind / And it lifts me to the sky."
— "To Be Around You", *Emotions*

caressing /kəˈresiNG/ *adjective*
gently touching, patting, or stroking a person or thing to show affection
"Every time, I feel the need / I envision you, caressing me."
— "The Roof", *Butterfly*

cascade /kaˈskād/ *noun*
a small waterfall, typically one of several that fall in stages down a steep rocky slope
"I'm picturing you and me there, right now / As the crystal cascades showered down."
— "Sunflowers for Alfred Roy", *Charmbracelet*

chanteuse /ˌSHänˈtoōz/ *noun*
a female singer of popular songs, especially in a concert or nightclub
"Lately, they've been calling me The Elusive Chanteuse."
"Me. I Am Mariah…The Elusive Chanteuse", *Me. I Am Mariah…The Elusive Chanteuse*

charade /SHəˈrād/ *noun*
a situation in which people pretend that something is true when it clearly is not
"Ever since you left me / I've been trying to hide the pain / Painting on a smile with lipstick / Putting on a big charade."
— "Circles", *The Emancipation of Mimi*

compulsively /kəmˈpəlsəvlē/ *adverb*
in a way that results from or relates to an irresistible urge
"Well, at first I didn't know / but now it's clear to me / You would cheat with all your freaks / and lie compulsively."
— "Shake It Off", *The Emancipation of Mimi*

conceal /kənˈsēl/ *verb*
keep (something) secret; prevent from being known or noticed
"I had a crush on you / Painstakingly, I would conceal the truth / You probably always knew."
— "Want You", *Glitter*

conceive /kənˈsēv/ *verb*
to form or devise (a plan or idea) in the mind
"Maybe now you just can't conceive / That there'll ever come a time when you're cold and lonely."
— "Someday", *Mariah Carey*

consequently /ˈkänsəkwən(t)lē/ *adverb*
as a result
"But I guess you wouldn't know that's the way I roll / Consequently, now your ego's fully overblown."
— "Clown", *Charmbracelet*

consumed /kənˈso͞omd/ *verb*
to use fuel, energy, time, or a product, *especially in large amounts*
"Everything is you / How can I pull through? / My heart is consumed / I'm so confused."
"Circles", *The Emancipation of Mimi*

contradicting /ˌkäntrəˈdik(t)iNG/ *verb*
denying the truth of (a statement) by asserting the opposite
"I don't wanna lose you to somebody else / But I can't go on contradicting myself."
— "Irresistible (West Side Connection)", *Charmbracelet*

convincingly /kənˈvinsiNGlē/ *adverb*
in a way that causes someone to believe that something is true or real
"Friends ask me how I feel / And I lie convincingly."
— "Breakdown", *Butterfly*

crescent /ˈkres(ə)nt/ *noun*
the shape of the visible part of the moon when it is less than half full
"A crescent moon began to shine / And I wanted to stay / Tangled up with you among the fireflies."
— "Fourth of July", *Butterfly*

crumbling /ˈkrəmb(ə)liNG/ *verb*
to break, or cause something to break, into small pieces
"Baby I need you now / Tonight I'm crumbling down
— "Long Ago", *Daydream*

delectable /dəˈlektəb(ə)l/ *adjective*
looking or tasting extremely good, and giving great pleasure
"Gimme some pure delectable love / Like I'm gonna give to you."
— "Bliss", *Rainbow*

delirium /dəˈlirēəm/ *noun*
an altered state of consciousness characterized by confusion, disorientation, and inability to think or remember clearly
"And when my sugar daddy takes me for a ride / Whatever way we go It's delirium time."
— "Loverboy", *Glitter*

delusional /dəˈlooZH(ə)nəl/ *adjective*
maintaining fixed false beliefs even when confronted with facts, usually as a result of mental illness
"You're delusional / You're delusional / Boy you're losing your mind."
— "Obsessed", *Memoirs of an Imperfect Angel*

demise /dəˈmīz/ *noun*
the end of something that was previously considered to be powerful
"Love without demise, oh, yes. He made it happen."
— "Sent From Up Above", *Mariah Carey*

demoralized /dəˈmôrəˌlīzd/ *adjective*
having lost confidence, enthusiasm or hope
"Pushing past the parasites / Down but not demoralized / Unconfined / But don't let go."
— "Portrait", *Caution*

denominator /dəˈnäməˌnādər/ *noun*
(In mathematics) *the* part of a fraction that is below the line, that indicates the number of equal parts into which the unit is divided
"Put all your shit in the elevator / It's goin' down like a denominator."
— "It's A Wrap", *Memoirs of an Imperfect Angel*

dependency /dəˈpend(ə)nsē/ *noun*
the state of relying on someone or something, especially when it is not normal or necessary

> ## "OH BABY, I'VE GOT A **DEPENDENCY** / ALWAYS STRUNG OUT FOR ANOTHER TASTE OF YOUR HONEY."
> — "Honey", *Butterfly*

desensitized /dē'sensə͵tīzd/ *adjective*
to cause someone to experience something, usually an emotion or a pain, less strongly than before
"*Somewhat desensitized. Still the same hopeful child. Haunted by those severed ties.*"
— "Portrait", *Caution*

desolate /'desələt/ *adjective*
(of a person) extremely sad and feeling alone
"*See, I was so desolate before you came to me.*"
— "Thank God I Found You", *Rainbow*

despair /də'sper/ *noun*
the complete loss or absence of hope
"*You just laugh as I drown in despair.*"
— "You're So Cold", *Emotions*

desperation /͵despə'rāSH(ə)n/ *noun*
a strong feeling of sadness, fear, and loss of hope
"*Carried me through desperation / To the one that was waiting for me.*"
— "Vision of Love", *Mariah Carey*

despondency /də'spändənsē/ *noun*
a state of low spirits caused by loss of hope or courage.
"*A boy and girl befriended me / We're bonded through despondency.*"
— "Petals", *Rainbow*

destitute /'destə͵toot/ *adjective*
without the basic necessities of life; lacking money, food, a home, or possessions
"*And maybe then the future will be a time / Without war, destitution and sorrow.*"
— "There's Got To Be a Way", *Music Box*

devious /ˈdēvēəs/ *adjective*
behaving in a dishonest or indirect way, or trickingly, in order to get something
"You were devious and shady / Only trifling with me."
— "You Had Your Chance", *Charmbracelet*

diminishing /dəˈminiSHiNG/ *verb*
make (someone or something) seem less impressive or valuable
"When the shadows are closing in / And your spirit diminishing / Just remember you're not alone."
— "Anytime You Need a Friend", *Music Box*

disarming /ˌdisˈärmiNG/ *adjective*
removing or capable of removing hostility or suspicion by being charming
"Cause you're so disarming / I'm caught up in the midst of you / And I can not resist at all."
— "Heartbreaker", *Rainbow*

discern /dəˈsərn/ *verb*
to distinguish (someone or something) with difficulty by sight or with the other senses
"There are some times when I tried to discern our reality / Wish that I just could be somebody else if you talked to me."
— "Camouflage", *Me. I Am Mariah… The Elusive Chanteuse*

discontent /ˌdiskənˈtent/ *noun*
a feeling of unhappiness or disapproval with the present situation
"Filled with discontent / Finding you can't quench."
"Thirsty", *Me. I Am Mariah… The Elusive Chanteuse*

discreetly /dəˈskrētlē/ *adverb*
in a way that is careful not to cause embarrassment or attract too much attention, especially by keeping something secret
"She didn't notice as you turned / And you discreetly winked your eye."
— "Secret Love", *The Emancipation of Mimi (Ultra Platinum Edition)*

disenchanted /ˌdisənˈCHan(t)əd/ *adjective*
disappointed by someone or something previously respected or admired
"*You took my love for granted / You left me lost and disenchanted.*"
— "GTFO", *Caution*

disillusion /ˌdisəˈlo͞oZH(ə)n/ *verb*
to cause (someone) to realize that a belief or an ideal is false
"*I don't want another pretender / To disillusion me one more time.*"
— "Dreamlover", *Music Box*

displaced /disˈplāsd/ *verb*
to cause (something or someone) to move from its proper or usual place
"*A displaced little girl / Wept years in silence / And whispered wishes you'd materialize.*"
— "Reflections (Care Enough)", *Glitter*

dissipate /ˈdisəˌpāt/ *verb*
to cause (something) to gradually weaken, spread out and disappear

> **"I LEFT THE WORST UNSAID / LET IT ALL DISSIPATE / AND I TRY TO FORGET."**
> — "Close My Eyes", *Butterfly*

dissuade /dəˈswād/ *verb*
to advise (someone) not to take a particular course of action
"*All my friends say I'm wastin' my time on you / Tryin' to dissuade me with schemes.*"
— "4Real 4Real", $E=MC^2$

distraught /dəˈstrôt,dəˈsträt/ *adjective*
extremely worried, nervous, or upset
"When you get caught in the rain with nowhere to run / When you're distraught and in pain without anyone."
— "Through The Rain", *Charmbracelet*

diversion /dəˈvərZHən,dīˈvərZHən/ *noun*
an activity that diverts the mind from tedious or serious concerns
"I never knew if I could believe in you / I thought I was just a diversion."
— "Now That I Know", *Music Box*

dominion /dəˈminyən/ *noun*
a territory, usually of considerable size, in which a single rulership holds absolute power
"I'm making a statement of my own opinion / Just a brief little reminder to help myself remember / I no longer live in your dominion."
— "The Art of Letting Go", *Me. I Am Mariah…The Elusive Chanteuse*

downhearted /ˌdounˈhärdəd/ *adjective*
discouraged; in low spirits
"If you really need me / Baby, just reach out and touch me / You don't ever have to be downhearted again."
— "Subtle Invitation", *Charmbracelet*

dutifully /ˈdo͞odəf(ə)lē/ *adverb*
in a way that is required by moral or legal obligation, societal or cultural expectations, or a person's position or occupation
"So many I considered closest to me / Turned on a dime and sold me out dutifully."
— "Petals", *Rainbow*

ecstasy /ˈekstəsē/ *noun*
an overwhelming feeling of great happiness or joyful excitement
"Like a taste of ecstasy / All I need is him to be my loverboy"
— "Loverboy", *Glitter*

effervescent /ˌefərˈves(ə)nt/ *adjective*
active, positive, and full of energy
"Childlike and effervescent with a well of pain."
— "Twister", *Glitter*

effortlessly /ˈefərtləslē/ *adverb*
in a manner requiring no physical or mental exertion
"You can fall into me / Once again effortlessly."
— "Subtle Invitation", *Charmbracelet*

elated /əˈlādəd/ *adjective*
extremely happy and excited
"You know you got me / Starry eyed and elated."
— "You Got Me", *Charmbracelet*

elude /əˈloōd/ *verb*
to escape, either physically or mentally
"Boy, I'm entangled up in you / These feelings I just can't elude."
"You Got Me", *Charmbracelet*

elusive /əˈloōsiv/ *adjective*
difficult to find, catch, or achieve
"I can't be elusive with you, honey / 'cause it's blatant that I'm feeling you."
— "Honey", *Butterfly*

emanating /ˈeməˌnātiNG/ *verb*
to flow out, issue, or proceed, as from a source or origin
"Like fireflies emanating the light / Just you and I universally tied."
— "Runway", *Caution*

emancipation /əˌmansəˈpāSH(ə)n/ *noun*
the fact or process of being set free from legal, social, or political restrictions
"It's a special occasion / Mimi's emancipation."
—"It's Like That", *The Emancipation of Mimi*

emblazoned /əmˈblāz(ə)nd,emˈblāz(ə)nd/ *verb*
to print or decorate on a surface in a very noticeable way

> *"I CAN SEE YOU CLEARLY / VIVIDLY EMBLAZONED IN MY MIND."*
> — "My All", *Butterfly*

embracing /əmˈbrāsiNG/ *verb*
hold closely in one's arms, especially as a sign of affection
"Everybody's smiling / The whole world is rejoicing / And everyone's embracing except for you and I."
— "Miss You Most (At Christmas Time)", *Merry Christmas*

empathy /ˈempəTHē/ *noun*
the ability to understand and emotionally share the feelings of another
"And it's the strongest thing I've ever experienced / So sorry, what ever happened to empathy?"
— "O.O.C.", *E=MC²*

enamored /iˈnamərd,eˈnamərd/ *verb*
to be filled with a feeling of love for
"Have you ever felt so enamored, baby? / That's how much I love you."
— "How Much", *Rainbow*

endlessly /ˈen(d)ləslē/ *adverb*
in a way that has or seems to have no limit or conclusion
"So many times / You keep me waiting around endlessly."
— "You're So Cold", *Emotions*

enfold /inˈfōld,enˈfōld/ *verb*
to closely hold or completely cover someone or something
"Come lay me down / Enfold me in your arms."
— "Babydoll", *Butterfly*

enmity /ˈenmədē/ *noun*
the state or feeling of being actively opposed or hostile to someone or something
"And after all these years of enmity, envy and tears / It's a shame you don't know me at all."
— "Languishing", *Memoirs of an Imperfect Angel*

enraptured /inˈrapCHərd,enˈrapCHərd/ *verb*
to be filled with great delight or joy; to fascinate or captivate

> *"I WAS SO **ENRAPTURED** / NO SENSIBILITY TO OPEN MY EYES."*
> — "Vanishing", *Mariah Carey*

entangled /inˈtaNGg(ə)ld,enˈtang(ə)ld/ *verb*
To become twisted together with or caught in
"Boy, I'm entangled up in you / These feelings I just can't elude."
— "You Got Me", *Charmbracelet*

entwined /ənˈtwīnd,enˈtwīnd/ *verb*
to be twisted and tangled or weaved together
"Delicately lay entwined / In an intimate daze."
— "Fourth of July", *Butterfly*

envelops /ɪnˈveləps/ *verb*
to wrap up in or as in a covering
"When you talk to me in that sensual tone / It envelops me and I lose my self-control."
— "Melt Away", *Daydream*

envision /ənˈviZH(ə)n/ *verb*
imagine as a future possibility; visualize
"Every time I feel the need / I envision you caressing me."
— "The Roof", *Butterfly*

essentially /əˈsen(t)SHəlē/ *adverb* used to emphasize the basic, fundamental, or intrinsic nature of a person, thing, or situation
"Essentially, you're all I'm living for / Basically, each day I need you more."
— "How Much", *Rainbow*

euphoric /yo͞oˈfôrik/ *adjective*
characterized by or feeling intense excitement and happiness
"It's a shame to be so euphoric and weak / When you smile at me."
— "Heartbreaker", *Rainbow*

everlasting /ˌevərˈlastiNG/ *adjective*
lasting forever or a very long time
"And it seemed everlasting / That you would always be mine."
— "Always Be My Baby", *Daydream*

evidently /ˈevəd(ə)ntlē/ *adverb*
in a way that is clearly seen or understood
"Evidently, your words were merely lies / Reverberating in my ears."
— "The Art of Letting Go", *Me. I Am Mariah… The Elusive Chanteuse*

exceedingly /ikˈsēdiNGlē/ *adverb*
to an advanced or unusual degree
"Letting go ain't easy / Oh, it's exceedingly hurtful."
— "The Art of Letting Go", *Me. I Am Mariah… The Elusive Chanteuse*

fair-weather /ferˈweT͟Hər/ *adjective*
weakening or failing in time of trouble
"Farewell, fair-weather friend / Abandonment returns to taunt me again."
— "I Only Wanted", *Charmbracelet*

falter /ˈfôltər/ *verb*
to start to lose strength or momentum
"I refuse to falter in what I believe / Or lose faith in my dreams."
— "Can't Take That Away (Mariah's Theme)", *Rainbow*

fantasize /ˈfan(t)əˌsīz/ *verb*
to indulge in daydreaming about something desired
"See, I used to be so shy / Sit at home and fantasize."
— "Your Girl", *The Emancipation of Mimi*

fathom /ˈfaTHəm/ *noun*
to thoroughly understand a difficult problem or an enigmatic person
"I couldn't have fathomed I would ever be without your love."
— "We Belong Together", *The Emanicipation of Mimi*

fervid /ˈfərvəd/ *adjective*
intensely enthusiastic or passionate, especially to an excessive degree
"Breathless and fervid / Amid the dandelions."
— "Fourth of July", *Butterfly*

flailing /flāliNG/ *verb*
to wave or swing or cause to wave or swing wildly
"She started flailing in the wind / Like golden petals scattering."
— "Petals", *Rainbow*

flaxen /ˈflaks(ə)n/ *adjective*
(especially of hair) of the pale yellow color
"Thank you for embracing a flaxen-haired baby / Although I'm aware you had your doubts."
— "Sunflowers for Alfred Roy", *Charmbracelet*

flourish /ˈflɔriSH/ *verb*
(of a person, animal, or other living organism) grow or develop in a healthy or vigorous way, especially as the result of a particularly favorable environment

> *"I HAVE LEARNED THAT BEAUTY HAS TO **FLOURISH** IN THE LIGHT."*
> — "Butterfly", *Butterfly*

foreseen /fôrˈsē,fərˈsē/ *verb*
to realize or understand something in advance or before it happens
"And who could've foreseen, in you I'd find the place I belonged forever."
— "Lead The Way", *Glitter*

fruitless /ˈfro͞otləs/ *adjective*
failing to achieve the desired results
"But it's all a big charade / And it's a fruitless game to play."
— "Slipping Away", *The Rarities*

futile /ˈfyo͞odl/ *adjective*
incapable of producing any useful result
"Make futile resolution / That I'm gonna let you be."
— "When I Feel It" (Unreleased), *The Emancipation of Mimi*

grapple /ˈgrap(ə)l/ *verb*
engage in a close fight or struggle without weapons
"She was kind of fragile and she had a lot to grapple with."
— "Twister", *Glitter*

gratitude /ˈgradəˌto͞od/ *noun*
the feeling or quality of being thankful
"I'm overwhelmed with gratitude / 'Cause baby, I'm so thankful I found you."
— "Thank God I Found You", *Rainbow*

gravitated /ˈɡravəˌtātəd/ *verb*
move toward or be attracted to a place, person, or thing
"I gravitated towards a patriarch / So young, predictably."
— "Petals", *Rainbow*

grotto /ˈɡrädō/ *noun*
a small cave, especially one that is made to look attractive
"We can make love in Italy in the grotto."
— "More Than Just Friends", *Memoirs of an Imperfect Angel*

guise /ɡīz/ *noun*
an external form, appearance, or manner of presentation, typically concealing the true nature of something
"Underneath the guise of a smile / Gradually I'm dying inside."
— "Breakdown", *Butterfly*

harbors /ˈhärbərz/ *verb*
to keep (a thought or feeling, typically a negative one) in one's mind, especially secretly
"She smiles through a thousand tears, and harbors adolescent fears."
— "Looking In", *Daydream*

hastily /ˈhāstəlē/ *adverb*
with excessive speed or urgency; hurriedly
"Before you act so hastily / Baby remember you need me."
— "You Need Me", *Mariah Carey*

haze /hāz/ *noun*
a state of mental obscurity or confusion
"You love me more than you love sunny summer days / And even more than you love floating in a haze."
— "You Don't Know What To Do", *Me. I Am Mariah… The Elusive Chanteuse*

heady /ˈhedē/ *adjective*
having a strong or exhilarating effect

> *"AND WE DRIFTED TO ANOTHER PLACE AND TIME / AND THE FEELING WAS SO **HEADY** AND SUBLIME."*
> — "Underneath The Stars", *Daydream*

hectic /ˈhektik/ *adjective*
characterized by intense agitation, excitement, confused and rapid movement
"Oh, when you walk by every night / Talking sweet and looking fine / I get kind of hectic inside."
— "Fantasy", *Daydream*

helplessly /ˈhelpləslē/ *adverb*
Without the ability to react actively
"Helplessly, I fell so deep / I was so naïve to let you in."
— "And You Don't Remember", *Emotions*

immersed /iˈmərsd/ *verb*
involve oneself deeply in a particular activity or interest.
"Ain't it a sweet, luscious delight / When you're immersed in my / Ocean of love, coming on strong."
— "Bliss", *Rainbow*

immortalized /i(m)ˈmôrdl‚īzd/ *verb*
to cause someone or something to be remembered for a very long time
"Cause we had a love / That won't be immortalized."
— "You Don't Know What To Do", *Me. I Am Mariah... The Elusive Chanteuse*

imprudently /imˈproōdntlē/ *adverb*
lacking discretion, wisdom, or good judgment
"Imprudently, I left every cell in me so naked / Somewhere at the core of you, blares our song."
— "Cry", *Me. I Am Mariah... The Elusive Chanteuse*

inadvertently /ˌinədˈvərtn(t)lē/ *adverb*
in a way that is not intentional
"'Cause you're so captivating / that I inadvertently / Always catch myself thinking 'bout / The things you do."
— "You Got Me", *Charmbracelet*

incandescent /ˌinkənˈdes(ə)nt/ *adjective*
emitting intense light as a result of being heated
"Glittering lights / Incandescent eyes / Still preserved in my mind."
— "Never Too Far", *Glitter*

incessantly /inˈsesn(t)lē/ *adverb*
continuing without stopping

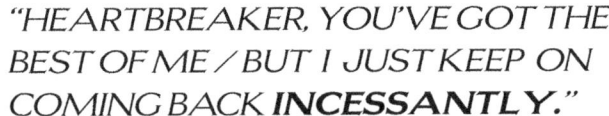

> *"HEARTBREAKER, YOU'VE GOT THE BEST OF ME / BUT I JUST KEEP ON COMING BACK **INCESSANTLY**."*
> — "Heartbreaker", *Rainbow*

indefinitely /inˈdef(ə)nətlē/ *adverb*
for an unlimited or unspecified period of time
"You'll always be a part of me / I'm part of you, indefinitely."
— "Always Be My Baby", *Daydream*

inevitably /inˈevədəblē, iˈnevtəblē/ *adverb*
in a way that cannot be avoided
"But inevitably you'll be back again / 'Cause you know in your heart, babe / Our love will never end."
— "Always Be My Baby", *Daydream*

inferior /inˈfirēər/ *adjective*
lower in rank, status, or quality
"Felt inferior inside / Until my saving grace shined on me."
— "My Saving Grace", *Charmbracelet*

inferiority /inˌfirēˈôrədē/ *noun*
the condition of being lower in status or quality than another or others
"See my inferiority complex kicks in /And the words escape me / And I'm paralyzed."
— "I Wish You Knew", *The Emancipation of Mimi*

inferno /inˈfərnō/ *noun*
a large fire that is dangerously out of control
"And once we lit this towering inferno / The flame keeps burning higher hotter we go."
— "One Mo' Gen", *Caution*

inherently /inˈhirəntlē,inˈherəntlē/ *adverb*
in a permanent, essential, or characteristic way
"Inherently, it's just always been strange."
— "Outside", *Butterfly*

insecurity /ˌinsəˈkyo͝orədē/ *noun*
uncertainty or anxiety about oneself
"She wades in insecurity and hides herself inside of me."
— "Looking In", *Daydream*

inseparable /inˈsepərəb(ə)l/ *adjective*
incapable of being disjoined
"Thought we'd stay together always and forever / But now I see that no one is inseparable."
— "Inseparable", *Memoirs of an Imperfect Angel*

insincere /ˌinsənˈsir/ *adjective*
not expressing genuine feelings
"He was so insincere / Now you're laying up in bed every night singing."
— "Thanx 4 Nothin'", *E=MC²*

intangible /inˈtanjəb(ə)l/ *adjective*
unable to be touched or grasped; not having physical presence
"So intangible, just like an echo / Still try and pretend it's possible / To bring us back to life."
— "Faded", *Me. I Am Mari*

intimacy /ˈin(t)əməsē/ *noun*
close familiarity or friendship
"You had my trust and intimacy / But you threw it away, just threw it away."
— "Did I Do That?", *Rainbow*

intimated /ˈin(t)əˌmātəd/ *verb*
to state or express indirectly
"You should've never intimated we were lovers / When you know very well / We never even touched each other."
— "Clown", *Charmbracelet*

intoxicated /inˈtäksəkādəd/ *adjective*
drunk or under the influence of drugs
"I'm in love / I'm alive / Intoxicated / Flying high."
— "Emotions", *Emotions*

intrinsic /inˈtrinzik/ *adjective*
being an extremely important and basic characteristic of a person or thing
"Like you'll always be an intrinsic part of me / Even though life goes on."
— "Subtle Invitation", *Charmbracelet*

irregardless /ˌirəˈgärdləs/ *adverb*
despite; not being affected by something
"Irregardless of what transpired / It ain't even worthy of a slick reply."
— "A No No", *Caution*

irreversibly /ˌi(r)rəˈvərsəblē/ *adverb*
in a way that cannot be undone or altered
"Irreversibly, falling in between / And it's hard / To be understand as you are."
— "Outside", *Butterfly*

languishing /ˈlaNGgwiSHiNG/ *adjective*
failure to make progress or be successful for a long period of time

> *"I WAS WONDERING, WOULD YOU REACH FOR ME / IF YOU SAW THAT I WAS **LANGUISHING?**"*
> — "Languishing (Interlude)", *Memoirs of an Imperfect Angel*

levity /ˈlevədē/ *noun*
humor or lack of seriousness, especially during a serious occasion
"Nah, you ain't seeing things / Or hallucinating / I brings that levity."
— "I'm That Chick", *E=MC²*

liability /ˌlīəˈbilədē/ *noun*
the state of being responsible for something, especially by law
"You're just trifling / nothing more than a liability."
— "The Art of Letting Go", *Me. I Am Mariah…The Elusive Chanteuse*

limitless /ˈlimətləs/ *adjective*
without end, limit, or boundary
"If it was me that was by your side / Limitless, without no rules."
— "8th Grade", *Caution*

linger /ˈliNGgər/ *verb*
to stay in a place longer than necessary because of a reluctance to leave
"And we'll linger on / Times can't erase a feeling this strong."
— "Always Be My Baby", *Daydream*

lullaby /ˈlələˌbī/ *noun*
a soothing song or piece of music intended to help a child go to sleep
"But I just can't walk away from paradise / So I guess I'll sing you that sweet lullaby."
— "Lullaby", *Charmbracelet*

majestically /məˈjestək(ə)lē/ *adjective*
in a way that is beautiful, powerful, or causes great admiration and respect
"*The sweet prince of peace / Lay majestically asleep, glorious and pure.*"
— "One Child", *Merry Christmas II You*

marionette /ˌmerēəˈnet/ *noun*
a puppet whose arms, legs and head are moved by strings that are attached
"*Who's gonna love you when your bankroll runs out? (A marionette show)*"
— "Clown", *Charmbracelet*

masquerade /ˈmaskəˌrād/ *noun*
a party, dance, or other festive gathering of persons wearing masks and other disguises
"*I was caught in your masquerade / Wish I'd stayed beneath my veil.*"
— "I Only Wanted", *Charmbracelet*

materialize /məˈtirēəˌlīz/ *verb*
to become fact; to happen as expected

> "A DISPLACED LITTLE GIRL WEPT YEARS IN SILENCE / AND WHISPERED WISHES YOU'D **MATERIALIZE**."
> — "Reflections (Care Enough)", *Glitter*

mesmerize /ˈmezməˌrīz/ *verb*
to hold completely the attention or interest of someone
"*Something that you do mesmerizes me / Sets my body free.*"
— "To Be Around You", *Emotions*

migrate /ˈmīˌgrāt/ *verb*
to move from one part of something to another
"*Treat it as a holiday / 'Cause he's a wrap / Y'all know I had to migrate.*"
— "Migrate", $E=MC^2$

minuscule /ˈminəˌskyo͞ol/ *adjective*
extremely small; tiny
"If my shows of gratitude are miniscule inside your mind, sorry."
— "I Wish You Well", *E=MC²*

misrepresented /ˌmisˌreprəˈzentɪd/ *verb*
to describe falsely an idea, opinion, or situation
"If I ever misrepresented / My self-image, then I'm sorry."
— "It's A Wrap", *Memoirs of an Imperfect Angel*

muddle /ˈməd(ə)l/ *verb*
to think or act in a confused aimless way
"We all make mistakes sometimes/But we muddle through."
— "With You", *Caution*

muster /ˈməstər/ *verb*
to collect or assemble (a number or amount)
"Wondering, could I muster the strength to exist in the bitter cold?"
— "Camouflage", *Me. I Am Mariah...The Elusive Chanteuse*

nonchalant /ˌnänSHəˈlänt/ *adjective*
(of a person or manner) feeling or appearing casually calm and relaxed
"Well, I guess I'm trying to be nonchalant about it / And I'm going to extremes to prove I'm fine without you."
— "Breakdown", *Butterfly*

nostalgia /nəˈstaljə/ *noun*
a sentimental longing or wistful affection for the past, typically for a period or place with happy personal associations
"But that's your nostalgia though / Just for the nostalgia."
— "Dedicated", *Me. I Am Mariah...The Elusive Chanteuse*

nothingness /ˈnəTHiNGnəs/ *noun*
the lack of value, worth, meaning
"Stranded here in nothingness / With only tears and loneliness."
— "And You Don't Remember", *Emotions*

novelty /ˈnävəltē/ *noun*
the quality or state of being new, different, and interesting
"Who's gonna care when the novelty's over? / When the star of the show isn't you anymore."
— "Clown", *Charmbracelet*

oblivious /əˈblivēəs/ *adjective*
not aware of or not concerned about what is happening around one
"The one I spent a lifetime searching for was right here all the time / I was oblivious, so very out of touch."
— "I've Been Thinking About You", *Music Box*

obscure /əbˈskyo͝or/ *adjective*
not clearly understood or expressed
"Laughing, we hurried beneath the sky / To an obscure place to hide."
— "Underneath The Stars", *Daydream*

ominously /ˈämənəslē/ *adverb*
in a way that suggests that something unpleasant is likely to happen

> *"THUNDER CLOUDS HUNG AROUND SO THREATENINGLY, **OMINOUSLY** HOVERING."*
> — "Fourth of July", *Butterfly*

omnipresent /ˈämnəˌprez(ə)nt/ *adjective*
widely or constantly encountered; common or widespread
"Limitless, omnipresent, kind of love couldn't have guessed."
— "Angels Cry", *Memoirs of an Imperfect Angel*

overblown /ˌōvərˈblōn/ *adjective*
bigger or more important or impressive than it should be
"But I guess you wouldn't know that's the way I roll / Consequently, now your ego's fully overblown."
— "Clown", *Charmbracelet*

cast /ˈōvərˌkast/ *adjective*
(of the sky or weather) marked by a covering of gray clouds
"It was overcast that day / And I was feeling some kind of way."
— "Faded", *Me. I Am Mariah… The Elusive Chanteuse*

overflows /ˌōvərˈflōz/ *verb*
to be completely filled *with something* beyond the limits of an available space
"Imagining that you're taking it slow / And so tenderly 'til the feeling overflows."
— "Melt Away", *Daydream*

overwhelmed /ˌōvərˈ(h)welmd/ *verb*
to be buried or beneath a huge mass
"I'm overwhelmed with gratitude / 'Cause baby, I'm so thankful I found you."
— "Thank God I Found You", *Rainbow*

painstakingly /ˈpānˌstākiNGlē/ *adverb*
with great care and thoroughness
"I had a crush on you / Painstakingly I would conceal the truth."
— "Want You", *Glitter*

paralyzed /ˈperəˌlīzd/ *adjective*
(of a person or part of the body) partly or wholly incapable of movement
"See, my inferiority complex kicks in / And the words escape me and I'm paralyzed."
— "I Wish You Knew", *The Emancipation of Mimi*

patriarch /ˈpātrēˌärk/ *noun*
the male head of a family or tribe
"I gravitated towards a patriarch so young, predictably."
— "Petals", *Rainbow*

peculiar /pəˈkyo͞olyər/ *adjective*
strange or odd; unusual
"I've been thinking about you in the most peculiar way."
— "I've Been Thinking About You", *Music Box*

persevere /ˌpərsəˈvir/ *verb*
to continue making an effort to do or achieve something despite difficulties, failure, or opposition
"Baby, our love will always persevere /Anything you ever need / You know that I'll be right here."
— "Yours", *Charmbracelet*

persuasive /pərˈswāsiv/ *adjective*
ability to make someone want to do or believe a particular thing
"You're too persuasive, I can't take it."
— "So Lonely (One and Only Part II)", *The Emancipation of Mimi*

petrified /ˈpetrəˌfīd/ *adjective*
frightened into a state of immobility
"When glory days turn to stormy nights / You must have been so petrified — Didn't you?"
— "I Wish You Well", $E=MC^2$

predictably /prēˈdiktəblē/ *adverb*
in a way that can be known, seen, or expected in advance
"Why do you sit in silence on the other end? / 'Til I hang up, and you predictably call right back again?"
— "X-Girlfriend", *Rainbow*

preserved /prəˈzərvd/ *verb*
to maintain or keep alive (a memory or quality)
"A place in time / Still belongs to us / Stays preserved in my mind."
— "Never Too Far", *Glitter*

prevail /prēˈvāl/ *verb*
to be or prove superior in strength, power, or influence
"So keep pressing on steadfastly / And you'll find what you need to prevail."
— "Through The Rain", *Charmbracelet*

procrastinating /prəˈkrastəˌnātiNG/ *verb*
delaying or postponing action; put off doing something
"Obviously procrastinating just to be / Close to you a little longer now."
— "Stay The Night", *The Emancipation of Mimi*

pseudo /ˈso͞odō/ *adjective*
not actually but having the appearance of
"Seems like all I do is think about our pseudo-romance."
— "Thanx 4 Nothin'", *E=MC²*

rationalize /ˈraSHənlˌīz/ *verb*
attempt to explain or justify (one's own or another's behavior or attitude) with logical and likely reasons, even if these are not true or appropriate
"Picture you in my mind / And I can't seem to rationalize / the way we let it end / It don't make no sense."
— "Last Kiss", *E=MC²*

reassurance /ˌrēəˈSHo͝orəns/ *noun*
a statement or comment that removes someone's doubts or fears
"You don't gotta look for reassurance / 'Cause clearly you're the only one that's getting this."
— "How Much", *Rainbow*

recapture /rēˈkapCHər/ *verb*
to take something into your possession again
"If I could recapture / All of the memories / And bring them to life / Surely, I would."
— "Vanishing", *Mariah Carey*

regularities /ˌregyəˈlerədiz/ *noun*
Someone or something that exists or happens repeatedly in a fixed style or pattern
"Them other regularities / They can't compete with MC.
— "For The Record", *E=MC²*

reiterate /rēˈidəˌrāt/ *verb*
to say something again or a number of times, typically for emphasis or clarity
"Must I reiterate? / Can we pick up the pace?"
— "One Mo' Gen", *Caution*

rejoicing /rəˈjoisiNG/ *noun*
the act or feeling of showing great happiness about something
"Everybody's smiling / The whole world is rejoicing / And everyone's embracing / Except for you and I, baby."
— "Miss You Most (At Christmas Time)", *Merry Christmas*

relinquish /rəˈliNGkwiSH/ *verb*
To voluntarily give up something
"And you tell me things / That you know persuade me / To relinquish my love to you."
— "Heartbreaker", *Rainbow*

reluctantly /rəˈləktən(t)lē/ *adverb*
in an unwilling and hesitant way
"Reluctantly we said goodbye / And left our secret place so far behind."
— "Underneath The Stars", *Daydream*

rendered /ˈrendərd/ *adjective*
to cause somebody or something to be in a particular state or condition
"And I was rendered still / There were no words for me to find at all."
— "When I Saw You", *Daydream*

rendezvous /ˈrändāˌvoō/ *noun*
a meeting at an agreed time and place
"Cause if you run your mouth and brag about this secret rendezvous / I will hunt you down."
— "Touch My Body", *Memoirs of an Imperfect Angel*

resigned /rəˈzīnd/ *adjective*
to give up deliberately, without resistance
"I was resigned to spend my life / Within a maze of misery."
— "Petals", *Rainbow*

resounding /rɪˈzaʊndiNG/ *adjective*
to be loud, clear and unmistakable
"And my heart was pounding / My inner voice resounding / Begging me to turn away / But I just had to see your face to feel alive."
— "The Roof", *Butterfly*

revel /ˈrevəl/ *verb*
to take delight in
"Baby I've been waiting so long / Revel inside of paradise."
— "Bliss", *Rainbow*

reverberating /rəˈvərbəˌrātiNG/ *adjective*
be repeated several times as it is reflected off different surfaces
"Evidently your words were merely lies / Reverberating in my ears, and the echo won't subside."
— "The Art of Letting Go", *Me. I Am Mariah… The Elusive Chanteuse*

reverie /ˈrevəri/ *noun*
state of being pleasantly lost in one's thoughts; a daydream
"You and me in a cloud of reverie / Spin around inside my head unendingly."
— "Melt Away", *Daydream*

rhapsodize /ˈrapsəˌdīz/ *verb*
to speak or write about with great enthusiasm and delight.

> *"THOUGHTS RUN WILD AS I SIT AND RHAPSODIZE / PAINT PRETTY PICTURES OF WHAT I'D DO IF YOU WERE MINE."*
> — "Melt Away", *Daydream*

romanticized /rōˈman(t)əˌsīzd/ *verb*
to make something seem better or more appealing than it really is
"Foolishly I romanticized / Someone was saving my life for the first time."
— "I Only Wanted", *Charmbracelet*

salvation /salˈvāSH(ə)n/ *noun*
the act of saving from danger, sin or evil
"Oh, Jesus born on this day / He is our light and salvation."
— "Jesus Born On This Day", *Merry Christmas*

sensual /ˈsen(t)SHəwəl/ *adjective*
expressing or suggesting physical, especially sexual, pleasure or satisfaction
"When you talk to me in that sensual tone / It envelops me and I lose my self-control."
— "Melt Away", *Daydream*

serenity /səˈrenədē/ *noun*
the state of being calm, peaceful, and untroubled
"I thought we'd be forever and always / You were serenity, you took away the bad days."
— "Angels Cry", *Memoirs of an Imperfect Angel*

sheathed /SHēTHd/ *verb*
covered in a thick or protective layer of a substance
"And the ice that's sheathed around my heart / Unravels as he smiles."
— "Right To Dream", *Tennessee (Original Motion Picture Soundtrack)*

solace /ˈsaləs/ *noun*
comfort offered to one who is disappointed or grieving
"Still preserved in my mind / In the memories, I'll find solace."
— "Never Too Far", *Glitter*

solidarity /ˌsäləˈderədē/ *noun*
unity or agreement of feeling or action, especially among individuals with common interests and responsibilities
"I truly wanted solidarity / Still wearing my blinders back then."
— "I Wish You Well", *E=MC²*

solitude /ˌsaləˈtud/ *noun*
the state of being seclusion or isolation; alone
"I am thinking of you / In my sleepless solitude tonight."
— "My All", *Butterfly*

splendor /ˈsplɛndər/ *noun*
a quality that outshines the usual
"I envision you caressing me / And go back in time / To relive the splendor of you and I / On the rooftop that rainy night."
— "The Roof", *Butterfly*

spiraling /ˈspaɪrəliNG/ *adjective*
To show a continuous and dramatic increase; winding or circling motion
"I still cry baby / I'm spiraling over you and me."
— "Crybaby", *Rainbow*

stability /stəˈbɪlədi/ *noun*
the quality or characteristic of being firm and steadfast
"I've always longed for undividedness and sought stability"
— "Petals", *Rainbow*

steadfastly /ˈstɛdˌfastlē/ *adverb*
in a firm and resolute manner
"So keep pressing on steadfastly / And you'll find what you need to prevail."
— "Through The Rain", *Charmbracelet*

steadily /ˈstɛdəlē/ *adverb*
in a consistent and unwavering manner
"I can't pretend these tears aren't overflowing steadily."
— "Butterfly", *Butterfly*

stigmatized /ˈstɪgməˌtīzd/ *verb*
to describe or regard in a way that shows strong disapproval

> *"BEEN **STIGMATIZED** / BEEN BLACK AND WHITE / FELT INFERIOR INSIDE."*
> — "My Saving Grace", *Charmbracelet*

strewn /stroon/ *verb*
To be untidily spread by scattering over a surface
"Sparkling colors were strewn across the sky."
— "Fourth of July", *Butterfly*

subconscious /səb'känSHəs/ *adjective*
the part of the mind of which one is not fully aware but which influences one's actions and feelings
"My subconscious seems to weave itself around you."
— "Babydoll", *Butterfly*

subdued /səb'do͞od/ *adjective*
lacking in vitality, intensity, or strength
"Don't be subdued, say it out loud."
— "Bliss", *Rainbow*

sublime /sə'blaɪm/ *adjective*
of such excellence, grandeur, or beauty as to inspire great admiration or awe
"The feeling was so heady and sublime."
— "Underneath The Stars", *Daydream*

subside /səb'sīd/ *verb*
to become less intense, violent, or severe
"The hurt from the heartache would not subside."
— "Thank God I Found You", *Rainbow*

succumb /sə'kəm/ *verb*
fail to resist pressure, temptation, or some other negative force
"When you love someone so deeply / They become your life / It's easy to succumb / To overwhelming fears inside."
— "Butterfly", *Butterfly*

suppressed /sə'prɛst/ *adjective*
prevent the development, action, or expression of (a feeling, impulse, idea)
"And feelings surfaced I'd suppressed / For such a long, long time."
— "The Roof", *Butterfly*

supremacy /sə'preməsē/ *noun*
the quality or state of having ultimate power, authority, or status
"In another land they still believe / Color grants supremacy."
— "There's Got To Be A Way", *Mariah Carey*

surpasses /sər'pæsɪz / *verb*
be or do something to a greater degree
"Looking in someone else's eyes / What we have surpasses even paradise."
— "Sent From Up Above", *Mariah Carey*

surreal /sə'riəl/ *adjective*
very strange or unusual having the quality of a dream
"Suddenly you're here and it's so surreal / And I don't know what the deal"
— "For The Record", *E=MC²*

tangible /'tanjəb(ə)l/ *adjective*
capable of being handled or grasped both physically and mentally
"Couldn't love ever be / Something tangible and real?"
— "I Only Wanted", *Charmbracelet*

taunt /tônt/ *verb*
to provoke or challenge with mockery, contempt, or criticism
"Abandonment returns to taunt me again."
— "I Only Wanted", *Charmbracelet*

tenderly /'tendərlē/ *adverb*
in a gentle, loving, or kind manner
"Imagining that you're taking it slow / And so tenderly 'til the feeling overflows."
— "Melt Away", *Daydream*

tentatively /'ten(t)ədəvlē/ *adverb*
a hesitant or uncertain manner that may be changed later
"Tentatively kissed goodnight / And went separate ways."
— "Fourth of July", *Butterfly*

tragically /ˈtrajək(ə)lē/ *adverb*
in a way that involves or causes extreme distress or sorrow
"Shattered dreams, cut through my mind / Tragically, our love has died."
— "And You Don't Remember", *Emotions*

transcending /trænt'sɛndiNG/ *adverb*
something that goes further, rises above, or exceeds limitations

> *"SOFT HEAVENLY EYES GAZED INTO ME /*
> *TRANSCENDING SPACE AND TIME."*
> — "When I Saw You", *Daydream*

transpired /trænt'spaɪərd/ *verb*
to come about, happen, or occur
"Irregardless of what transpired / It ain't even worthy of a slick reply."
— "A No No", *Caution*

trepidation /tre-pə-ˈdā-shən/ *noun*
a feeling of fear or worry about what is going to happen
"She was full of such trepidation / There in front of the whole damn nation."
— "With You", *Caution*

trustingly /ˈtrʌstiNGli/ *adverb*
in a way that shows you are willing to believe that other people are good, honest
"Trustingly, I gave myself to you."
— "And You Don't Remember", *Emotions*

unbridled /ˈənˌbraɪdld/ *adjective*
not restrained or controlled
"Wild horses run unbridled or their spirit dies."
— "Butterfly", *Butterfly*

unburden /ˈənˌbərdn/ *verb*
to free or relieve oneself of something that is worrisome
"Unfailingly, I will return to your arms / And unburden your heart."
— "Forever", *Daydream*

uncertainty /ˌənˈsərtntē/ noun
the feeling of not being sure what will happen in the future
"But in your heart — uncertainty forever lies / And you'll always be / Somewhere on the outside."
— "Outside", *Butterfly*

unclouded /ˌənˈkloudəd/ adjective
not darkened or obscured
"You gave me a breath of life / Unclouded my eyes with sweet serenity."
— "I Am Free", *Daydream*

undeniably /ˌəndəˈnīəblē/ adverb
in a way that is certainly true
"The moments that we shared seem so very real, undeniably so."
— "Mesmerized", *The Rarities*

undisguised /ˌʌn.dɪsˈgaɪzd/ adjective
not concealed or hidden
"And you have opened my heart and lifted me inside / By showing me yourself, undisguised."
— "Whenever You Call", *Butterfly*

undividedness /ˌəndəˈvīdədnəs/ noun
the quality or state of being undivided
"I've always longed for undividedness and sought stability."
— "Petals", *Rainbow*

undressable /ˌənˈdresəbəl/ adjective
not capable of being clothed
"It's beautiful / Oh, you make me feel undressable."
— "#Beautiful", *Me. I Am Mariah...The Elusive Chanteuse*

unendingly /ʌnˈen.diNGli/ adverb
in a way that does not stop, or seems to have no end
"You and me in a cloud of reverie / Spin around inside my head unendingly."
— "Melt Away", *Daydream*

unfailingly / ˌənˈfāliNGlē / *adverb*
in a way that is reliable or unchanging at all times
"Unfailingly, I will return to your arms. And unburden your heart."
— "Forever", *Daydream*

unguided / ˌənˈgīdəd / *adjective*
not controlled or led in a particular path or direction
"Blind and unguided / Into a world divided."
— "Outside", *Butterfly*

unjustly / ˌənˈjəs(t)lē / *adverb*
in a manner that is not in accordance with what is right and fair
"My prince was so unjustly handsome."
— "GTFO", *Caution*

unloosed / ˌənˈlo͞ost / *verb*
to undo; let free
"Boy I'm all wrapped up in you / You make me feel so unloosed."
— "Ribbon", *Memoirs of an Imperfect Angel*

untimely / ˌənˈtīmlē / *adjective*
an event or act happening or done at an unsuitable or premature time
"When I think of our untimely end and everything we could have been / I cry, baby I cry."
— "Crybaby", *Rainbow*

unvarnished / ˌənˈvärniSHt / *adjective*
a statement or manner that is plain and straightforward

> "AFTER SO MUCH SUFFERING / I FINALLY FOUND **UNVARNISHED** TRUTH."
> — "Thank God I Found You", *Rainbow*

unwavering / ənˈwervəriNG / *adjective*
marked by firm determination or resolution
"All you need is to remain unwavering / In spite of the chains that bind you."
— "Triumphant (Get 'Em)", *Triumphant (The Remixes)*

unyielding /ˌənˈyēldiNG/ *adjective*
not likely to be swayed or give way to pressure; resolute
"Immediately, I pretended to be feeling similarly / And led you to believe I was okay / To just walk away from the one thing / That's unyielding and sacred to me."
— "Breakdown", *Butterfly*

uplifting /əpˈliftiNG/ *adjective*
Offering or providing happiness, optimism, or hope
"I need somebody uplifting / To take me away."
— "Dreamlover", *Music Box*

vanishing /ˈvaniSHiNG/ *verb*
to begin to disappear suddenly and completely
"You're vanishing, drifting away."
— "Vanishing", *Mariah Carey*

ventilation /ˌven(t)əˈlāSHən/ *noun*
the supply of air to the lungs by means of a machine or device used to support a person who cannot breathe easily on their own
"Gasping for air, I'm ventilation / You out of breath / Hope you ain't waiting."
— "Obsessed", *Memoirs of an Imperfect Angel*

verbalize /ˈvərbəˌlīz/ *verb*
to express (ideas or feelings) in words, especially by speaking out loud
"The way I feel for you, I can't describe / It's almost too intense to verbalize."
— "How Much", *Rainbow*

volcanic /välˈkanik/ *adjective*
a feeling or emotion of bursting out or liable to burst out violently
"You and me seems volcanic / Just like the stars and planets."
— "Say Something", *The Emancipation of Mimi*

vicinity /vəˈsinədē/ *noun*
an area near or surrounding a particular place
"It's too dangerous to be in the vicinity of where you are."
— "Betcha Gon' Know (The Prologue)", *Memoirs of an Imperfect Angel*

vividly /ˈvivədlē/ *adverb*
in a manner that produces powerful feelings or strong, clear images in the mind
"I can see you clearly / Vividly emblazoned in my mind."
— "My All", *Butterfly*

vulnerable /ˈvəlnər(ə)bəl/ *adjective*
liable to physical or emotional attack or harm
"I should have known that you'd go and break my heart / Knowing I was so vulnerable."
— "Vulnerability", *Rainbow*

wade /wād/ *verb*
to walk through water or another substance that offers resistance
"She wades in insecurity / And hides herself inside of me."
— "Looking In", *Daydream*

wakening /ˈweɪkənɪNG/ *noun*
the act of waking
"Only once in a lifetime love rushes in / Changing you with a tide and dawn's ribbon of light / Bursts through the dark / Wakening you inside."
— "When I Saw You", *Daydream*

wandering /ˈwɑndərɪNG/ *verb*
to travel about without any clear destination
"Late at night like a little child / Wandering around alone in my new friend's home."
— "Crybaby", *Rainbow*

wane /weɪn/ *verb*
decrease in vigor, power, or extent (especially of a condition or feeling)
"Every time you come back / My feelings start to wane."
— "When I Feel It" (Unreleased), *The Emancipation of Mimi*

wayward /ˈweɪwərd/ *adjective*
resistant to guidance or discipline
"I was a wayward child / With the weight of the world / That I held deep inside."
— "Close My Eyes", *Butterfly*

weakening /ˈwikɪniNG/ *verb*
to cause to become less strong, powerful, determined, or effective
"When you look at me / I go soft and cave in / And I can't conceal / That I'm slowly weakening."
— "Melt Away", *Daydream*

woeful /ˈwōfəl/ *adjective*
characterized by, expressive of, or causing sorrow or misery.
"I should've never listened to your woeful stories / The ones you probably told a thousand times before me."
— "Clown", *Charmbracelet*

> "WORDS HAVE MEANING AND THUS, THEY HAVE POWER."
>
> MARIAH CAREY

DISCOVERIES

Write down your favorite or new 'Mariahcabulary' words here.

WORD: _____

SONG TITLE: _____

DEFINITION: _____

_____

_____

LYRICS: _____

_____

_____

WORD: _____

SONG TITLE: _____

DEFINITION: _____

_____

_____

LYRICS: _____

_____

_____

WORD: _____

SONG TITLE: _____

DEFINITION: _____

_____

_____

LYRICS: _____

_____

_____

WORD: _____
SONG TITLE: _____
DEFINITION: _____
_____
_____

LYRICS: _____
_____
_____

WORD: _____
SONG TITLE: _____
DEFINITION: _____
_____
_____

LYRICS: _____
_____
_____

WORD: _____
SONG TITLE: _____
DEFINITION: _____
_____
_____

LYRICS: _____
_____
_____

WORD: _____
SONG TITLE: _____
DEFINITION: _____
_____
_____

LYRICS: _____
_____
_____
_____

WORD: _____
SONG TITLE: _____
DEFINITION: _____
_____
_____

LYRICS: _____
_____
_____
_____

WORD: _____
SONG TITLE: _____
DEFINITION: _____
_____
_____

LYRICS: _____
_____
_____

WORD: _____
SONG TITLE: _____
DEFINITION: _____
_____
_____

LYRICS: _____
_____
_____

WORD: _____
SONG TITLE: _____
DEFINITION: _____
_____
_____

LYRICS: _____
_____
_____

WORD: _____
SONG TITLE: _____
DEFINITION: _____
_____
_____

LYRICS: _____
_____
_____

WORD: _____
SONG TITLE: _____
DEFINITION: _____
_____
_____

LYRICS: _____
_____
_____

WORD: _____
SONG TITLE: _____
DEFINITION: _____
_____
_____

LYRICS: _____
_____
_____

WORD: _____
SONG TITLE: _____
DEFINITION: _____
_____
_____

LYRICS: _____
_____
_____

WORD: _____
SONG TITLE: _____
DEFINITION: _____
_____
_____

LYRICS: _____
_____
_____

WORD: _____
SONG TITLE: _____
DEFINITION: _____
_____
_____

LYRICS: _____
_____
_____

WORD: _____
SONG TITLE: _____
DEFINITION: _____
_____
_____

LYRICS: _____
_____
_____

WORD: _____
SONG TITLE: _____
DEFINITION: _____
_____
_____

LYRICS: _____
_____
_____

WORD: _____
SONG TITLE: _____
DEFINITION: _____
_____
_____

LYRICS: _____
_____
_____

WORD: _____
SONG TITLE: _____
DEFINITION: _____
_____
_____

LYRICS: _____
_____
_____

CITATIONS

Burrus, Kandi and Mariah Carey. "X-Girlfriend." *Rainbow*. Columbia, 1999. CD.

Carey, Mariah. "And You Don't Remember." *Emotions*. Columbia, 1991. CD.

Carey, Mariah. "Close My Eyes." *Butterfly*. Columbia, 1997. CD.

Carey, Mariah. "Inseparable." *Memoirs of an Imperfect Angel*. Island Def Jam, 2009. CD.

Carey, Mariah. "*Me. I Am Mariah… The Elusive Chanteuse.*" *Me. I Am Mariah… The Elusive Chanteuse*. Def Jam, 2014. CD.

Carey, Mariah. "Outside." *Butterfly*. Columbia, 1997. CD.

Carey, Mariah. "Outside." *Butterfly*. Columbia, 1997. CD.

Carey, Mariah. "Petals." *Rainbow*. Columbia, 1999. CD.

Carey, Mariah. "Thanx 4 Nothin'." $E=MC^2$. Island Def Jam, 2008. CD.

Carey, Mariah. "The Roof (Back in Time)." *Butterfly*. Columbia, 1997. CD.

Carey, Mariah. "Underneath The Stars." *Daydream*. Columbia, 1995. CD.

Carey, Mariah. "When I Feel It (Unreleased)." *The Emancipation of Mimi*. Island Def Jam, 2005. Digital.

Carey, Mariah and Barry White. "It's A Wrap." *Memoirs of an Imperfect Angel*. Island Def Jam, 2009. CD.

Carey, Mariah and Ben Marguilies. "Someday." *Mariah Carey*. Columbia, 1990. CD.

Carey, Mariah and Ben Marguilies. "Vanishing." *Mariah Carey*. Columbia, 1990. CD.

Carey, Mariah and Ben Marguilies. "Vision of Love." *Mariah Carey*. Columbia, 1990. CD.

Carey, Mariah and Bryan-Michael Cox. "4Real4Real (Bonus Track)." $E=MC^2$. Island Def Jam, 2008. CD.

Carey, Mariah and Bryan-Michael Cox. "For The Record." $E=MC^2$. Island Def Jam, 2008. CD.

Carey, Mariah and Daniel Moore II. "Portrait." *Caution*. Epic, 2018. CD.

Carey, Mariah and Dave "Jam" Hall. "Slipping Away." *Always Be My Baby / Slipping Away*. Columbia, 1996. CD Single.

Carey, Mariah and Dianne Warren. "Can't Take That Away (Mariah's Theme)." *Rainbow*. Columbia, 1999. CD.

Carey, Mariah and James "Big Jim" Wright. "Camouflage." *Me. I Am Mariah… The Elusive Chanteuse*. Def Jam, 2014. CD.

Carey, Mariah and James "Big Jim" Wright. "Circles." *The Emancipation of Mimi*. Island Def Jam, 2005. CD.

Carey, Mariah and James "Big Jim" Wright. "Cry." *Me. I Am Mariah… The Elusive Chanteuse*. Def Jam, 2014. CD.

Carey, Mariah and James "Big Jim" Wright. "Fly Like a Bird." *The Emancipation of Mimi*. Island Def Jam, 2005. CD.

Carey, Mariah and James "Big Jim" Wright. "I Wish You Knew." *The Emancipation of Mimi*. Island Def Jam, 2005. CD.

Carey, Mariah and James "Big Jim" Wright. "Languishing (The Interlude)." *Memoirs of an Imperfect Angel*. Island Def Jam, 2009. CD.

Carey, Mariah and Kanye West. "Stay The Night." *The Emancipation of Mimi*. Island Def Jam, 2005. CD.

Carey, Mariah and Kenneth "Babyface" Edmonds. "Melt Away." *Daydream*. Columbia, 1995. CD.

Carey, Mariah and Lionel Cole. "I Only Wanted." *Charmbracelet*. Island, 2002. CD.

Carey, Mariah and Lionel Cole. "Sunflowers for Alfred Roy." *Charmbracelet*. Island, 2002. CD.

Carey, Mariah and Lionel Cole. "Through The Rain." *Charmbracelet*. Island, 2002. CD.

Carey, Mariah and Loris Holland. "Mesmerized." *The Rarities*. Columbia/Legacy, 2020. CD.

Carey, Mariah and Marc Shaiman. "One Child." *Merry Christmas II You*. Island Def Jam, 2010. CD.

Carey, Mariah and Missy Elliott. "Babydoll." *Butterfly*. Columbia, 1997. CD.

Carey, Mariah and Philippe Pierre. "Reflections (Care Enough)." *Glitter*. Virgin Records, 2001. CD.

Carey, Mariah and Rhett Lawrence. "Sent From Up Above." *Mariah Carey*. Columbia, 1990. CD.

Carey, Mariah and Rhett Lawrence. "You Need Me." *Mariah Carey*. Columbia, 1990. CD.

Carey, Mariah and Ric Wake. "There's Got to Be a Way." *Music Box*. Columbia, 1993. CD.

Carey, Mariah and Rodney Jerkins. "The Art of Letting Go." *Me. I Am Mariah… The Elusive Chanteuse*. Def Jam, 2014. CD.

Carey, Mariah and Scram Jones. "Your Girl." *The Emancipation of Mimi*. Island Def Jam, 2005. CD.

Carey, Mariah and Swizz Beatz. "Secret Love." *The Emancipation of Mimi (Ultra Platinum Edition)*. Island Def Jam, 2005. CD.

Carey, Mariah and Walter Afanasieff. "Anytime You Need a Friend." *Music Box*. Columbia, 1993. CD.

Carey, Mariah and Walter Afanasieff. "Butterfly." *Butterfly.* Columbia, 1997. CD.

Carey, Mariah and Walter Afanasieff. "Forever." *Daydream.* Columbia, 1995. CD.

Carey, Mariah and Walter Afanasieff. "Fourth of July." *Butterfly.* Columbia, 1997. CD.

Carey, Mariah and Walter Afanasieff. "I Am Free." *Daydream.* Columbia, 1995. CD.

Carey, Mariah and Walter Afanasieff. "Jesus Born on This Day." *Merry Christmas.* Columbia, 1994. CD.

Carey, Mariah and Walter Afanasieff. "Lead The Way." *Glitter.* Virgin Records, 2001. CD.

Carey, Mariah and Walter Afanasieff. "Looking In." *Daydream.* Columbia, 1995. CD.

Carey, Mariah and Walter Afanasieff. "Miss Your Most (At Christmas Time)." *Merry Christmas.* Columbia, 1994. CD.

Carey, Mariah and Walter Afanasieff. "My All." *Butterfly.* Columbia, 1997. CD.

Carey, Mariah and Walter Afanasieff. "When I Saw You." *Daydream.* Columbia, 1995. CD.

Carey, Mariah and Walter Afanasieff. "Whenever You Call." *Butterfly.* Columbia, 1997. CD.

Carey, Mariah and Willie Nelson. "Right to Dream." *Tennessee Soundtrack.* Island Def Jam, 2008. Digital.

Carey, Mariah, et al. "#Beautiful." *Me. I Am Mariah… The Elusive Chanteuse.* Def Jam, 2014. CD.

Carey, Mariah, et al. "8th Grade." *Caution.* Epic, 2018. CD.

Carey, Mariah, et al. "A No No." *Caution.* Epic, 2018. CD.

Carey, Mariah, et al. "Always Be My Baby." *Daydream.* Columbia, 1995. CD.

Carey, Mariah, et al. "Angels Cry." *Memoirs of an Imperfect Angel.* Island Def Jam, 2009. CD.

Carey, Mariah, et al. "Betcha Gon' Know (The Prologue)." *Memoirs of an Imperfect Angel.* Island Def Jam, 2009. CD.

Carey, Mariah, et al. "Bliss." *Rainbow.* Columbia, 1999. CD.

Carey, Mariah, et al. "Breakdown." *Butterfly.* Columbia, 1997. CD.

Carey, Mariah, et al. "Clown." *Charmbracelet.* Island, 2002. CD.

Carey, Mariah, et al. "Crybaby." *Rainbow.* Columbia, 1999. CD.

Carey, Mariah, et al. "Dedicated." *Me. I Am Mariah… The Elusive Chanteuse.* Def Jam, 2014. CD.

Carey, Mariah, et al. "Did I Do That?" *Rainbow.* Columbia, 1999. CD.

Carey, Mariah, et al. "Dreamlover." *Music Box.* Columbia, 1993. CD.

Carey, Mariah, et al. "Faded." *Me. I Am Mariah… The Elusive Chanteuse*. Def Jam, 2014. CD.

Carey, Mariah, et al. "Fantasy." *Daydream*. Columbia, 1995. CD.

Carey, Mariah, et al. "GTFO." *Caution*. Epic, 2018. CD.

Carey, Mariah, et al. "Heartbreaker." *Rainbow*. Columbia, 1999. CD.

Carey, Mariah, et al. "Honey." *Butterfly*. Columbia, 1997. CD.

Carey, Mariah, et al. "How Much." *Rainbow*. Columbia, 1999. CD.

Carey, Mariah, et al. "I Wish You Well." *E=MC²*. Island Def Jam, 2008. CD.

Carey, Mariah, et al. "I'm That Chick." *E=MC²*. Island Def Jam, 2008. CD.

Carey, Mariah, et al. "I've Been Thinking About You." *Music Box*. Columbia, 1993. CD.

Carey, Mariah, et al. "Irresistible (West Side Connection)." *Charmbracelet*. Island, 2002. CD.

Carey, Mariah, et al. "It's Like That." *The Emancipation of Mimi*. Island Def Jam, 2005. CD.

Carey, Mariah, et al. "Last Kiss." *E=MC²*. Island Def Jam, 2008. CD.

Carey, Mariah, et al. "Long Ago." *Daydream*. Columbia, 1995. CD.

Carey, Mariah, et al. "Loverboy." *Glitter*. Virgin Records, 2001. CD.

Carey, Mariah, et al. "Lullaby." *Charmbracelet*. Island, 2002. CD.

Carey, Mariah, et al. "Migrate." *E=MC²*. Island Def Jam, 2008. CD.

Carey, Mariah, et al. "More Than Just Friends." *Memoirs of an Imperfect Angel*. Island Def Jam, 2009. CD.

Carey, Mariah, et al. "My Saving Grace." *Charmbracelet*. Island, 2002. CD.

Carey, Mariah, et al. "Never Too Far." *Glitter*. Virgin Records, 2001. CD.

Carey, Mariah, et al. "Now That I Know." *Music Box*. Columbia, 1993. CD.

Carey, Mariah, et al. "O.O.C." *E=MC²*. Island Def Jam, 2008. CD.

Carey, Mariah, et al. "Obsessed." *Memoirs of an Imperfect Angel*. Island Def Jam, 2009. CD.

Carey, Mariah, et al. "One and Only." *The Emancipation of Mimi*. Island Def Jam, 2005. CD.

Carey, Mariah, et al. "One Mo' Gen." *Caution*. Epic, 2018. CD.

Carey, Mariah, et al. "Ribbon." *Memoirs of an Imperfect Angel*. Island Def Jam, 2009. CD.

Carey, Mariah, et al. "Runway (Bonus Track)." *Caution*. Epic, 2018. CD.

Carey, Mariah, et al. "Say Something." *The Emancipation of Mimi*. Island Def Jam, 2005. CD.

Carey, Mariah, et al. "Shake It Off." *The Emancipation of Mimi*. Island Def Jam, 2005. CD.

Carey, Mariah, et al. "So Lonely (One and Only Part II)." *The Emancipation of Mimi (Platinum Edition)*. Island Def Jam, 2005. CD.

Carey, Mariah, et al. "Subtle Invitation." *Charmbracelet*. Island, 2002. CD.

Carey, Mariah, et al. "Thank God I Found You." *Rainbow*. Columbia, 1999. CD.

Carey, Mariah, et al. "Thirsty." *Me. I Am Mariah… The Elusive Chanteuse*. Def Jam, 2014. CD.

Carey, Mariah, et al. "To Be Around You." *Emotions*. Columbia, 1991. CD.

Carey, Mariah, et al. "Touch My Body." *E=MC²*. Island Def Jam, 2008. CD.

Carey, Mariah, et al. "Triumphant (Get 'Em)." *Triumphant (The Remixes)*. Island Def Jam, 2012. CD.

Carey, Mariah, et al. "Twister." *Glitter*. Virgin Records, 2001. CD.

Carey, Mariah, et al. "Vulnerability (Interlude)." *Rainbow*. Columbia, 1999. CD.

Carey, Mariah, et al. "Want You." *Glitter*. Virgin Records, 2001. CD.

Carey, Mariah, et al. "We Belong Together." *The Emancipation of Mimi*. Island Def Jam, 2005. CD.

Carey, Mariah, et al. "You Don't Know What to Do." *Me. I Am Mariah… The Elusive Chanteuse*. Def Jam, 2014. CD.

Carey, Mariah, et al. "You Got Me." *Charmbracelet*. Island, 2002. CD.

Carey, Mariah, et al. "You Had Your Chance." *Charmbracelet*. Island, 2002. CD.

Carey, Mariah, et al. "You're So Cold." *Emotions*. Columbia, 1991. CD.

Carey, Mariah, et al. "Yours." *Charmbracelet*. Island, 2002. CD.

Davis, Michaela Angela. *The Meaning of Mariah Carey*. Andy Cohen Books. 2023.

Dictionary.com, 2025, https://www.dictionary.com. Accessed 3 Nov. 2025.

"Mariah Carey." Wikipedia, Wikimedia Foundation, 25 March 2025, https://en.m.wikipedia.org/wiki/Mariah_Carey

Mariah Carey. Genius, 2024, genius.com/artists/Mariah-carey.

"Mariah Carey on How to Write Lyrics." MasterClass, 5 Jan 2023, https://www.masterclass.com/articles/mariah-carey-on-how-to-write-lyrics.

"Mariah Carey Genius Level: The Full Interview on Her Iconic Hits & Songwriting Process." YouTube, uploaded by Genius, 16 November 2018, https://youtu.be/rdMQ31DlTjg?si=_p3hQx-LawajKbjX

Merriam-Webster's Collegiate Dictionary, 11th ed., 2004.

Merriam-Webster, www.merriam-webster.com. Accessed 3 Nov. 2025.

ABOUT THE AUTHOR

Byron McCray Miller is an award-winning illustrator, author, and journalist from Brooklyn, New York, whose work is deeply rooted in music, storytelling, and cultural preservation. A lifelong devotee of rhythm and blues, he co-hosts the podcast *90's R&B University* and authored the celebrated children's book *90's R&B — A to Z*. His artistic talent earned him the 2024 Jane Addams Peace Association Children's Book Award for his illustrations in *A Song for the Unsung: Bayard Rustin, the Man Behind the 1963 March on Washington*. When not creating, Byron enjoys life in Connecticut with his husband and son.

Made in United States
North Haven, CT
05 May 2025

68571918R00036